Red Animals

by Teddy Borth

ABDO
ANIMAL COLORS
Kids

abdopublishing.com

Published by Abdo Kids, a division of ABDO, PO Box 398166, Minneapolis, Minnesota 55439.

Copyright © 2015 by Abdo Consulting Group, Inc. International copyrights reserved in all countries.
No part of this book may be reproduced in any form without written permission from the publisher.

Printed in the United States of America, North Mankato, Minnesota.

102014

012015

 THIS BOOK CONTAINS
RECYCLED MATERIALS

Photo Credits: iStock, Science Source, Shutterstock, Thinkstock,

Production Contributors: Teddy Borth, Jennie Forsberg, Grace Hansen

Design Contributors: Candice Keimig, Laura Rask, Dorothy Toth

Library of Congress Control Number: 2014943668

Cataloging-in-Publication Data

Borth, Teddy.

 Red animals / Teddy Borth.

   p. cm. -- (Animal colors)

ISBN 978-1-62970-697-9 (lib. bdg.)

Includes index.

1. Animals--Juvenile literature.   I. Title.

590--dc23

                    2014943668

Table of Contents

Red

Red is a **primary color**.
Red cannot be made
by mixing other colors.

Mixing Colors

🔴 **+** 🟡 **=** 🟠

🟡 **+** 🔵 **=** 🟢

🔴 **+** 🔵 **=** 🟣

🟠 **+** 🟢 **+** 🟣 **=** ⚫

Primary Colors

🔴 **Red**

🟡 **Yellow**

🔵 **Blue**

Secondary Colors

🟠 **Orange**

🟢 **Green**

🟣 **Purple**

5

Red on Land

Red foxes have great hearing.

They can hear a mouse squeak

from 330 feet (100 m) away.

6

7

A mandrill is an ape. The males have red faces. The leader has the most red on his face.

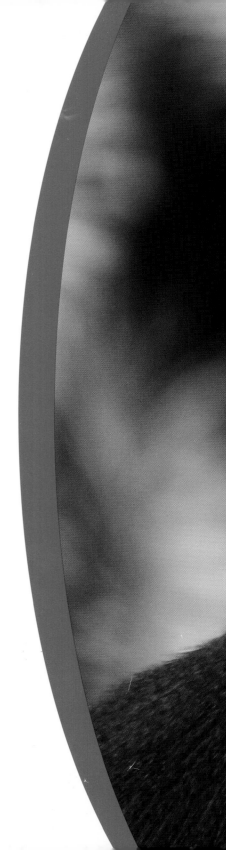

9

Red pandas are found

in China. A red panda

is the size of a house cat.

Roosters have red on their heads. This is called the **comb**. Healthy roosters have bright combs.

13

Red in Air

The scarlet ibis starts out
gray, brown, or white. Scarlet
ibises eat lots of **shrimp**.
This is why they turn red!

14

Red lily beetles eat plants.
They leave many plants
destroyed. Gardeners
do not like these beetles!

Red in Water

Frogfishes live on the ocean floor. They use their fins to walk. They change color to hide in rocks and plants.

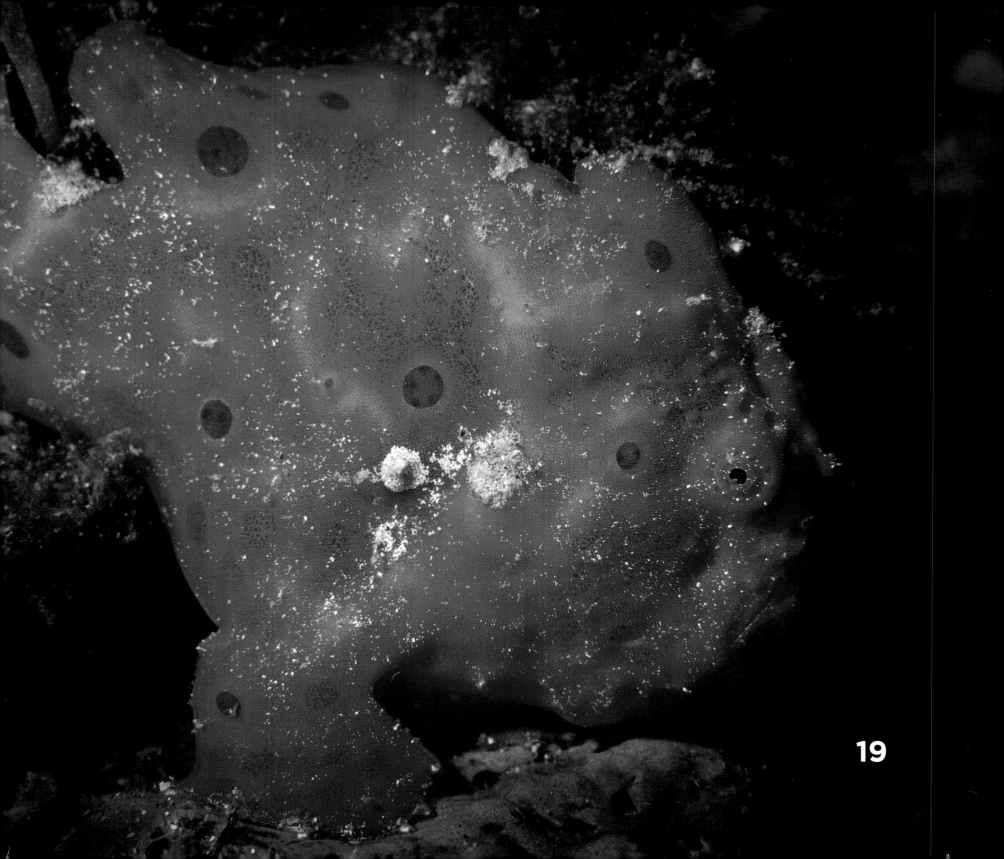

19

Acadian redfish swim

in the Atlantic Ocean.

They swim near Canada.

They can live up to 75 years.

21

More Facts

- Red is the first color to have a name after black and white.

- Dogs and cattle cannot see red or green.
  They see gray instead.

- Red is the color of anger, heat, courage,
  love, celebration, and danger.

Glossary

comb – the patch of red that looks like hair on the head of a rooster.

primary color – a color that cannot be made by mixing other colors.

secondary color – a color resulting from mixing two primary colors.

shrimp – a tiny ocean animal that looks like a small lobster.

Index

abdokids.com

Use this code to log on to abdokids.com and access crafts, games, videos, and more!

Abdo Kids Code:
ARK6979

24